STEER WRESTLING

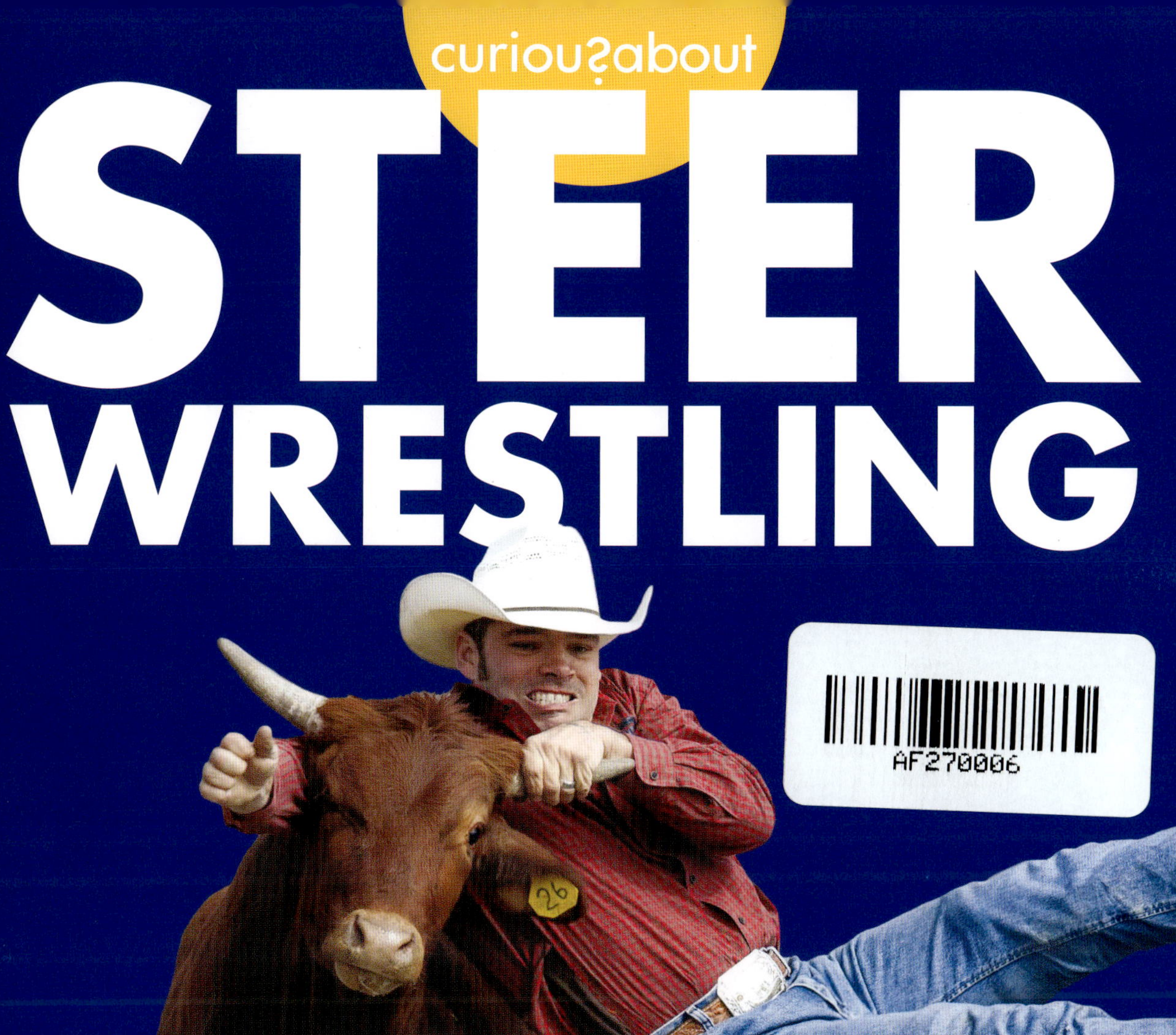

BY RACHEL GRACK

What are you

curious about?

Curious About is published by
Amicus Learning, an imprint of Amicus
P.O. Box 227, Mankato, MN 56002
www.amicuspublishing.us

Editors: Megan Siewert and Ana Brauer
Series Designer: Kathleen Petelinsek
Book Designer and Photo Researcher: Kathleen Petelinsek

Library of Congress Cataloging-in-Publication Data
Names: Koestler-Grack, Rachel A., 1973– author.
Title: Curious about steer wrestling / by Rachel Grack.
Description: Mankato, MN : Curious About is published by Amicus
Learning, [2025] | Series: Curious about Rodeo | Includes
bibliographical references and index. | Audience: Ages 6–9
years | Audience: Grades 2–3 | Summary: "Learn how cowboys
and cowgirls (and their horses) compete in steer wrestling rodeo
events in this question-and-answer book for elementary-aged
readers. Includes infographics and back matter to support research
skills along with table of contents, glossary, books and websites
for further research, and index"— Provided by publisher.
Identifiers: LCCN 2024015029 (print) |
LCCN 2024015030 (ebook) |
ISBN 9798892000888 (lib bdg) |
ISBN 9798892001465 (paperback) |
ISBN 9798892002042 (ebook)
Subjects: LCSH: Steer wrestling—Juvenile literature.
Classification: LCC GV1834.45.S73 K64
2025 (print) | LCC GV1834.45.S73 (ebook) |
DDC 791.8/4—dc23/eng/20240509
LC record available at https://lccn.loc.gov/2024015029
LC ebook record available at https://lccn.loc.gov/2024015030

Photo Credits: Alamy Stock Photo/BYphoto, 11, Ed Endicott, 2,
17, Photography By Marco, 7, Xinhua, cover, 1; Dreamstime/
Dtfoxfoto, 3, 20–21, Pierre Jean Durieu, 18–19, Rico Leffanta,
6; Shutterstock/archivector, 8, Christopher Halloran, 12–13,
Diane Garcia, 2, 9, Jim Parkin, 17, Kobby Dagan, 4–5, Unique
Design Team, 8; Wikimedia Commons/Skarabeusz, 14–15

Printed in China

What is steer wrestling?

Rodeos give cowboys and cowgirls a chance to show off their roping and riding skills.

It's a timed rodeo sport. Two cowboys on horseback chase down a **steer**. The hazer rides along its right side and guides it to the bulldogger. The bulldogger slides off his galloping horse and **wrestles** the steer to the ground. The fastest time wins!

Can women do it?

A cowgirl competes in steer undecorating.

Professional bulldoggers are mostly men. There are some women who work as hazers. Ladies compete in steer undecorating instead. The events are similar. But ladies do not dismount. The rider leans off her saddle. She reaches for the steer's back. She pulls off a ribbon and holds it high.

Steer undecorating
takes excellent balance
and riding skills.
THROW DOWN!

How hard is steer wrestling?

Very hard! The steer weighs two times more than the cowboy. Bulldoggers need to be very strong to throw one down. They both reach 30 miles per hour (48 kilometers per hour) during the chase. It takes speed, balance, and exact timing. There is no room for mistakes. Riders must be super quick to win.

ON THE SCALE: BULLDOGGER VS. STEER

Bulldoggers have to do a lot of weight training to be strong enough to wrestle a steer.

CHAPTER TWO

Is the steer running loose?

No. It starts in the **chute**. The hazer and bulldogger back their horses into the **box**. They nod. The steer is released. It charges into the arena. The steer has a head start. The cowboys race from the box.

The steer runs
out of the chute
once the gate
is opened.

THE EVENT

What happens in the arena?

The bulldogger charges toward the steer. He rides up close. Meanwhile, the hazer keeps the steer running straight ahead. The bulldogger reaches down as he slides off the saddle. He hooks his right arm under the right horn. He grabs the left horn with his other hand. Time to throw it down!

How does he throw down the steer?

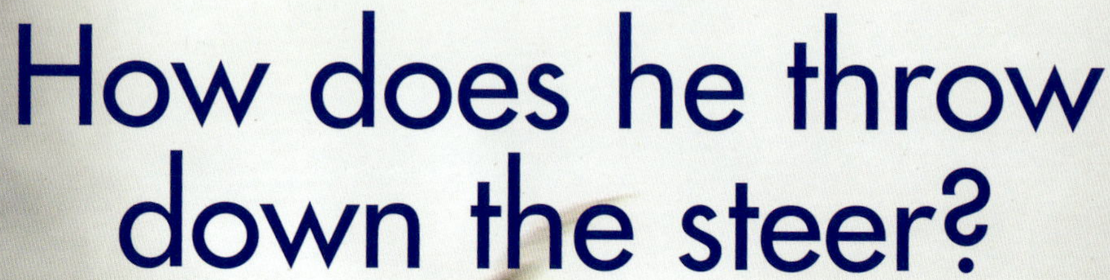

DID YOU KNOW? The first bulldoggers would bite the steer's upper lip to help take it down. Today, no biting is allowed! Cowboys stick to power and mighty force.

The bulldogger digs his heels into the dirt. This slows the steer. He twists its head and pulls it down. It lands on its side. One more pull on the horns. The body turns. Now all four feet point in the same direction. Stop the clock!

Steer wrestling is jokingly called "throwing beef." Can you figure out why?

Does the steer get hurt?

Fair question! These steers can handle rough-housing. They are **bred** to be sturdy. They are trained for the job. Steers are used to being around people. This lessens their stress in the ring. Yes, they could get hurt. But rodeo vets help keep them safe and healthy.

HOW VETS KEEP STEERS SAFE

Check that the animals are healthy enough to perform.

Treat animals if they get hurt.

Inspect arenas and pens to make sure they are safe.

Watch for injuries.

Steers often wear horn wraps for extra padding.

CHAPTER THREE

3

Are there rules?

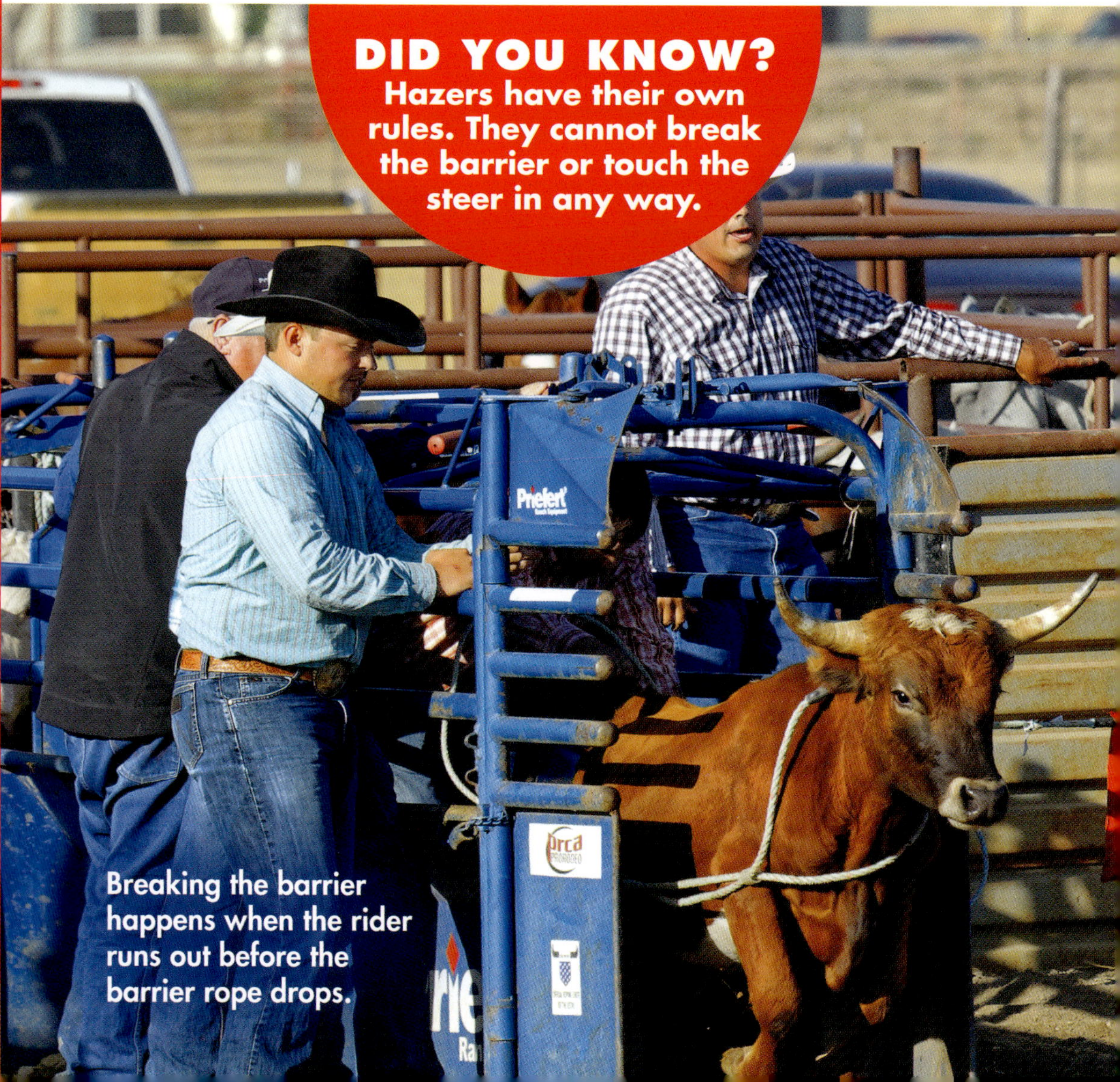

DID YOU KNOW?
Hazers have their own rules. They cannot break the barrier or touch the steer in any way.

Breaking the barrier happens when the rider runs out before the barrier rope drops.

A few. First, riders must be patient. They need to give the steer its head start. Breaking the barrier adds 10 seconds to their time. Next, the steer must be thrown down. It might trip or get knocked over. The rider must let it get back up. Otherwise, he gets **disqualified**.

When does the clock stop?

When the steer is flat on its side. And its nose and feet are pointed in the same direction. Steer wrestling is a timed event. Riders get 30 seconds. But the pros do it in under five. Times are often a hundredth of a second apart. The fastest time wins. They score a "no time" if the steer gets away.

ASK MORE QUESTIONS

Can kids wrestle steers?

How much money do steer wrestlers make?

Try a BIG QUESTION: Would I rather be a bulldogger or a hazer?

SEARCH FOR ANSWERS

Search the library catalog or the Internet.
A librarian, teacher, or parent can help you.

Using Keywords
Find the looking glass.

Keywords are the most important words in your question.

If you want to know:
- about steer wrestling for kids, type: YOUTH STEER WRESTLING
- about steer wrestler winnings, type: STEER WRESTLING PAYOUTS

FIND GOOD SOURCES

Here are some good, safe sources you can use in your research.
Your librarian can help you find more.

Books

Bull Riding
by Rachel Grack, 2025.

Tie-Down Roping
by Rochelle Groskreutz, 2020.

Internet Sites

Kiddle: Bill Pickett Facts for Kids
https://kids.kiddle.co/Bill_Pickett
Kiddle is an online encyclopedia for kids. Search for information on a wide variety of educational topics. Learn about the cowboy who started the sport of steer wrestling.

Britannica: Steer Wrestling
https://www.britannica.com/sports/steer-wrestling
Britannica is an encyclopedia with educational information on many topics. Learn more about rodeos and steer wrestling.

SHARE AND TAKE ACTION

Watch steer wrestling.
Ask an adult to help you find videos of steer wrestling.

Try wrestling with a friend.
Make rules to keep it friendly. Imagine how hard it would be to wrestle a steer!

Attend a rodeo.
Catch the quick throw down in person!

box The pen where riders back their horses into for a timed rodeo event.

bred To mate animals together to produce certain characteristics.

chute A pen that holds animals in position so riders can safely mount.

disqualified To be taken out of a competition for breaking a rule.

professional Someone who participates in a sport for money.

steer Male cattle that cannot reproduce.

wrestles To struggle with and try to throw down an opponent.

About the Author

Rachel Grack has been writing children's nonfiction for twenty-five years. She lives on a ranch in the heart of rodeo country (southern Arizona). Some evenings, she wanders over to watch her neighbors in friendly roping competitions. A western restaurant in town offers weekly bull riding and mutton busting. But Rachel much prefers a quiet ride on her gentle paint horse, Lady.